Original title:
All the Love You Carry

Copyright © 2024 Swan Charm Publishing
All rights reserved.

Editor: Jessica Elisabeth Luik
Author: Olivia Orav
ISBN HARDBACK: 978-9916-86-126-4
ISBN PAPERBACK: 978-9916-86-127-1

Canvas of the Soul

Upon the canvas pure and white,
Colors blend, a vivid sight.
Brushstrokes whisper tales untold,
In dreams and hues, a world unfolds.

Expression flows through vibrant streams,
Captured moments, silent dreams.
In every shade, emotions dance,
Revealing secrets at a glance.

The artist's hand, a guiding light,
Transforms the night into the bright.
A masterpiece, a living scroll,
A story on the canvas of the soul.

Harmony of Hearts

In the silence of the dawn,
Hearts unite, a gentle bond.
Whispers of an ancient song,
In love's embrace, we belong.

Each beat a note in life's grand score,
A symphony forevermore.
Through trials, triumphs, and despair,
In harmony, we share and care.

The melody of souls entwined,
In love's pure light, we are defined.
Together strong, never apart,
A timeless harmony of hearts.

Radiant Whispers

In twilight's glow, the whispers rise,
A dance of stars in velvet skies.
Soft murmurs of the night unfold,
Secrets of the moonlight told.

Each whisper, a celestial flare,
A glimpse of dreams floating in air.
In radiant whispers, shadows play,
Guiding souls along their way.

The night reveals its gentle might,
In whispers through the silent night.
A luminous embrace so tender,
Radiant whispers, pure surrender.

Veins of Affection

Through every vein, affection flows,
A silent balm for unseen woes.
In love's embrace, a tender trace,
A comfort found in every place.

Connections deep, unseen but felt,
In every heartbeat, ties are knelt.
Through joys and sorrows, love remains,
Flowing gently through our veins.

The pulse of love, a steady beat,
In every moment, pure and sweet.
Affection's veins, a lifeline strong,
Binding hearts where they belong.

Canvas of Emotion

On the canvas of emotion, painted shades so deep,
Colors blend in chaos, where secrets softly sleep.
Brushes dipped in longing, sweep across the heart,
Every stroke a whisper, of feelings torn apart.

Hues of joy and sorrow, merge in twilight's glow,
Mystery in shadows, truths we cannot show.
Within the artist's silence, vibrant dreams reside,
Each creation speaks, no words can ever hide.

In the gallery of passion, echoes find their way,
Silent screams of heartache, in twilight's soft ballet.
The masterpiece of life, framed in memories bright,
Held in the warmth of hope, wrapped in love so tight.

Echoes of Devotion

In the quiet drifts of dawn, devotion softly sings,
Echoes through the morning mist, on faith's gentle wings.
Whispers of the sacred, fill the humble air,
Every breath a prayer, in love's eternal care.

Beyond the silent twilight, stars begin to gleam,
Promise held in constellations, faith begins to dream.
Serenade of moonlight, guides the weary soul,
In the heart of night, devotion makes us whole.

In the shadows of the past, vows forever stand,
Unbroken chains of promise, clasped within our hand.
Through the chimes of history, love will always trace,
Echoes of devotion, in every time and place.

Garden of Sentiments

In the garden of sentiments, petals softly kiss,
Morning dew of memories, yields a tender bliss.
Every bloom a story, tales of love and pain,
Whispers in the fragrance, dancing in the rain.

Beneath the velvet sky, where wishes softly fall,
Dreams grow in the twilight, sheltered by the wall.
Branches weave in silence, cradling the night,
Sanctuary of the heart, in the soft moonlight.

Blossoms of forgiveness, weave a tapestry,
Threads of hope and sorrow, stitching destiny.
In the garden's silence, secrets softly blend,
Sentiments in bloom, journeys without end.

Melody of Mirth

In the melody of mirth, laughter reigns so free,
Notes of joy and happiness, dance in harmony.
Tunes of pure delight, ripple through the air,
Light and sweet as morning, consequence unaware.

Through the grassy meadows, glee begins to play,
Whistling winds of fortune, chase the tears away.
Beats of carefree moments, echo down the lane,
Every smile a symphony, curing heart's disdain.

Rhythms of tomorrow, sung in joyful tone,
Every step in wonder, never felt alone.
The melody of mirth, carried through the years,
A song of endless laughter, drying all our tears.

Whispers in the Dark

In the quiet of the night,
Where shadows softly glide,
Dreams take their silent flight,
Beyond where fears abide.

Stars whisper secrets deep,
In the realms unseen,
Night's embrace we keep,
In a tranquil, moonlit scene.

Hush, the darkness speaks,
In murmurs soft and true,
Through twilight's gentle peaks,
We find a world anew.

Echoes of the past,
Linger in the air,
In shadows they are cast,
Whispered without a care.

In whispers, we confide,
Surrendering the stark,
Embracing what we hide,
In whispers in the dark.

Tender Pages

In the quiet of the dawn,
When morning light first gleams,
Upon the pages drawn,
Lie the tenderest of dreams.

Each word a gentle kiss,
Each line a lover's sigh,
In the book of tender bliss,
Our hearts learned to fly.

Memories etched in ink,
Stories of our days,
And as each page we link,
Love weaves its warm embrace.

Through trials and through joys,
In sorrow and in mirth,
Our tale endures the noise,
Rooted deep in earth.

Tender pages hold,
The essence of our song,
In their story told,
We find where we belong.

Fountain of Heartbeats

In a garden lush and green,
A fountain gently flows,
With heartbeats felt unseen,
In rhythm it bestows.

The pulse of life it bears,
In waters clear and bright,
Each droplet softly shares,
The song of day and night.

From deep within it springs,
Boundless joy and grace,
With every beat it sings,
A love time can't erase.

Ripples dance and play,
Upon the mirrored pool,
In every heart they stay,
Eternal, bright, and cool.

This fountain ever gleams,
In the core of hearts entwined,
Where love's pure sunlight beams,
A legacy unconfined.

Threads of Affection

Woven through our days,
In colors bright and bold,
Are threads in tender ways,
By love's own hand extolled.

Each strand a story starts,
Of journeys we have known,
Knitting together hearts,
In patterns we have sewn.

Through laughter and through tears,
These threads we'll intertwine,
Binding our hopes and fears,
In a tapestry divine.

The fabric of our lives,
Crafted with such care,
In every thread survives,
Affection pure and rare.

And as the years unfold,
This woven love we'll see,
In threads of warmth and gold,
Our hearts remain as free.

Eclipsed in Warmth

In twilight's gentle, softened glide,
Shadows dance where whispers hide,
A moonlit veil on dreams bestowed,
Eclipsed in warmth, where hearts have flowed.

Embrace the night, let worries wane,
Stars above sing sweet refrain,
The sky's a canvas dark and wide,
On this path, let love abide.

Golden hues in midnight's core,
Silent secrets, yearning lore,
Hold the warmth, let darkness be,
In eclipse, our spirits free.

The night, a blanket, tender, true,
Holds the whispers, shades of blue,
With every beat, a story fanned,
In warmth eclipsed, we understand.

Stars of the Heart

In the quiet of the night,
Hearts aglow with gentle light,
Stars of love in sky so vast,
Moments shared, forever last.

Twinkling tales and silent vows,
Life's true compass, where love allows,
Eyes alight with dreams untold,
Stars of the heart, brave and bold.

Cosmic ballet in endless grace,
Love's sweet echo in each space,
Boundless bonds, through time they start,
Lighting up the stars of heart.

Each heartbeat holds a spark,
Guiding souls through paths and lark,
In the dark, they softly chart,
The endless stars that bind the heart.

Vivid Embrace

Colors burst in morning's dawn,
Life renews with each awn,
Vivid hues in every face,
Wrapped in nature's warm embrace.

Petals whisper, leaves revere,
Scenes of splendor drawing near,
In this palette, love is traced,
Blissful, bold in vivid embrace.

Meadows paint with every hue,
In the light, a heart rings true,
Each new day, a canvas grace,
Life, a vast and vivid embrace.

Moments shimmer, softly stay,
In our hearts, a bright array,
Feel the world, its tender place,
Held within this vivid embrace.

Fields of Kindness

In vast fields where kindness grows,
Every gentle wind that blows,
Sows the seeds of love and care,
Fields of kindness, pure and fair.

Tender hands and hearts unite,
Guiding souls through dark and light,
Every act, a bloom to share,
Kindness flowing everywhere.

Paths of peace in meadows green,
Every smile, a healing scene,
In this place, all hearts repair,
Fields of kindness, scent the air.

Boundless skies above the land,
In these fields, we understand,
Love's soft touch, beyond compare,
In fields of kindness, hearts grow rare.

Tender Cargo

Soft whispers sail through twilight's glow,
In gentle arms, where dreams bestow,
A lullaby by moonlight's crest,
For tender cargo, hearts caressed.

In cradle's sway, the night does wane,
With starlight weaving love's refrain,
Beneath the sky, in quiet grace,
A journey's start in this embrace.

Through fields of time, with steps so light,
Their future gleams like morning bright,
Each breath a promise, softly told,
In tender cargo, lives unfold.

And in the hush of night's embrace,
The world slows down, a peaceful place,
For here they rest, both young and old,
With tender cargo, dreams unfold.

The Pulse of Affinity

Beneath the stars, we find our way,
In shadows cast, where friendships sway,
A silent drum of hearts aligned,
The pulse of affinity refined.

Through laughter's echo, whispers clear,
With every beat, we draw more near,
In bonds unseen, yet felt so true,
Our souls entwine in rhythm's view.

From dawn's first light to twilight's end,
Through every trial, we transcend,
With hands held fast, we face the tide,
In pulse of life, we do confide.

No words can bind what hearts have spun,
This tether strong, as we are one,
For in the dance of time and space,
The pulse of affinity, we chase.

Burden of Bliss

In love's warm glow, a heavy cloak,
The burden sweet, no words provoke,
A joy so vast, it weighs the heart,
In blissful bonds, we feel the start.

With every touch, a deeper trace,
The lines of life on hands and face,
Through trials shared and dreams embraced,
The burden of bliss in moments laced.

In quiet nights, our secrets told,
As hearts entwine, both young and old,
We carry forth this splendid weight,
In burden of bliss, our twined fate.

For bliss demands a heart that's true,
To bear its weight, it takes just two,
In every kiss, the balance lies,
The burden of bliss, forever ties.

Hues of Heartfelt

In colors bright, our love does bloom,
With every shade, dispelling gloom,
A canvas wide where feelings flow,
In hues of heartfelt, we both grow.

From deepest reds to softest dawn,
Each stroke a whisper, tightly drawn,
Our palette mixed with joy and strife,
In hues of heartfelt, paints our life.

Through seasons change, our colors blend,
A masterpiece that knows no end,
In every tint, a memory piqued,
The hues of heartfelt, ever sleek.

Beneath the sky, our shades align,
Creating art where hearts entwine,
For in this love, the spectrum lies,
In hues of heartfelt, endless skies.

Underneath the Surface

Beneath the waves where darkness lies,
The hidden world begins to rise,
With whispered tales and secret cries,
In depths unknown, a treasure prize.

Where shadows dance in silent grace,
And mysteries in every place,
The sea holds wonders to embrace,
A world unseen, a silent space.

Amidst the coral's vibrant hues,
Where life in every crevice brews,
A realm that's ancient, ever true,
Beneath the surface, life renews.

Everlasting Embrace

In arms that hold when times are dire,
With love that burns, a constant fire,
We find our peace, our hearts' desire,
An everlasting, pure aspire.

Through storms and sun, in joy and pain,
Together facing life's refrain,
The bond we share shall e'er remain,
An endless love in heart and vein.

A touch, a glance, a whispered word,
In quiet moments, love is stirred,
A dance of souls, as yet unheard,
In everlasting embrace unfurled.

Laden with Kindness

A simple smile, a helping hand,
In acts of grace, we understand,
The world's a kinder, softer land,
When kindness guides and love's at hand.

Through gentle words and caring eyes,
We lift the heart, the spirit flies,
In generous acts, the beauty lies,
A world transformed, no more disguise.

Each day a chance to be the light,
To ease a burden, make it right,
With kindness, hearts are ever bright,
A world of warmth within our sight.

The Depth of Grace

In times of trial, hearts seek rest,
In depths of grace, the soul is blessed,
With courage found, and fears confessed,
In grace, we find our spirits dressed.

Amidst the darkest night of fear,
A light of grace can still appear,
It whispers softly, always near,
A balm for sorrow, wiping tears.

Through grace, we rise above the strife,
It breathes new hope into our life,
With love and peace, it ends the strife,
And fills our hearts, with grace, we thrive.

A Heartful Journey

Through boundless skies, our dreams will weave,
Two souls entwined by fate's decree,
With every step, our hearts believe,
In paths unknown, our spirits free.

Mountains high and valleys deep,
We wander far, where shadows creep,
Guided by love's eternal sweep,
Together strong, in joy we'll leap.

Whispers of the wind call out,
In timeless mystery, they shout,
A journey blessed by heartfelt clout,
In love's embrace, there's no doubt.

Stars above, a guiding light,
Through darkest hours of the night,
With courage bold, we'll win the fight,
For love's true path is ever bright.

Hand in hand, our stories told,
In warmth and trust, hearts unfold,
A timeless bond, forever bold,
A journey shared, worth more than gold.

Echoes of Affection

Soft echoes of affection ring,
Across the vast and endless sea,
In whispered tones, our spirits sing,
A melody of you and me.

In twilight's glow, our love we find,
A tender touch, a gentle gaze,
With every beat, two hearts aligned,
Together through life's winding maze.

Moonlit nights and sunlit days,
We walk in sync, in perfect cheer,
Through joy and pain, in countless ways,
Affection's song we hold so dear.

Every glance and spoken word,
Resonates with feelings true,
In silence felt, our love is heard,
A bond as strong as morning dew.

In echoes soft, affection thrives,
A symphony of hearts combined,
Through life's great dance, our love survives,
A timeless echo, soul-defined.

The Weight of Tenderness

In fields of gold where breezes play,
The weight of tenderness we bear,
In every touch and gentle sway,
A silent vow, beyond compare.

With whispered words and soulful eyes,
Our hearts convey what lips can't speak,
In moments shared, no need for guise,
A tender bond, both strong and meek.

Through trials harsh and moments sweet,
We shoulder burdens, light and vast,
In tenderness, our spirits meet,
Creating memories meant to last.

Under the stars, the night unfolds,
Soft murmurs float on moonlit air,
In tender acts, love's truth it holds,
A sacred pledge, both pure and rare.

In every tear and joyous grin,
The weight of tenderness is shown,
A testament to love within,
A bond that's forever known.

Embrace of the Soul

In dawn's first light, two souls embrace,
A love that's pure and deeply true,
In whispered breaths, we find our place,
A bond as vast as skies of blue.

With every heartbeat, moments shared,
In silent nights and stormy days,
In every struggle, love declared,
An endless dance in heartfelt ways.

Eyes that speak without a sound,
Hands that hold with gentle might,
In soul's embrace, our love is found,
A beacon bright in darkest night.

Through life's expanse, our paths align,
Together strong, we face the storm,
With every step, our hearts entwine,
In love's embrace, forever warm.

Eternal flame that lights our way,
A love that time cannot control,
In every night and every day,
We cherish the embrace of the soul.

Whispers of the Heart

In the silent night, the stars align,
Soft whispers weave through hearts entwine.
A melody of love, so pure, so sweet,
In quiet moments, two souls meet.

Beneath the moon's soft, guiding light,
Two spirits dance in silent flight.
A love that's felt, though words unspoke,
In tender whispers, hearts awoke.

The breeze that moves through leaves of gold,
Speaks secrets of the hearts, untold.
In every rustle, whispers build,
A tapestry of love fulfilled.

The silent echoes of the past,
In whispers, hold the moments vast.
From dusk 'til dawn, they gently rise,
A symphony beneath the skies.

In heart's deep corners, whispers play,
A song that time will not decay.
In quiet spaces, love imparts,
The endless whispers of our hearts.

Unseen Emotions

Beyond the gaze, emotions hide,
In silent realms, they softly bide.
A world within where feelings flow,
In shadows, unseen, they grow.

A tear unshed, a smile unseen,
In hidden corners, feelings glean.
Beneath the surface, currents strong,
Unseen emotions, silent song.

The facades we wear, the masks in place,
Hide the storm in each soft grace.
In depths unknown, where secrets keep,
Unseen emotions silently seep.

In moments lost, in times alone,
Emotions speak in silent tone.
Words unspoken, yet deeply felt,
In unseen realms, they softly melt.

A whisper here, a glance that stays,
Emotions dance in shadowed ways.
In silent depths, they find their part,
The unseen whispers of the heart.

Gentle Burdens

In quiet hours, the burdens lie,
Soft whispers in the evening sky.
They weigh with grace, a gentle touch,
A silent load, yet felt so much.

Upon the shoulders, light they rest,
These gentle burdens, unconfessed.
Though softly held, they shape our day,
In whispered tones, they find their way.

In every step, a silent weight,
They whisper truths, articulate.
Though unseen, they firmly cling,
In gentle burdens, hearts take wing.

The silent sigh, the weary gaze,
They speak of burdens, quiet haze.
In shadows deep, they softly sing,
The gentle burdens life can bring.

In tender moments, burdens ease,
Their whispers carried by the breeze.
In each soft touch, they fade to art,
The gentle burdens of the heart.

Silent Devotion

In dawn's first light, devotion wakes,
In silence, all our love remakes.
No need for words, the soul's refrain,
In quiet, our devotion plain.

Through every day, in calm we tread,
With silent vows and paths we've led.
In every heartbeat, every glance,
Our silent devotion finds its chance.

The quiet strength, a love that's pure,
In silence, all our hearts endure.
With every breath, a promise made,
In silent devotion, unafraid.

No need to speak, the love is clear,
In every look, the soul draws near.
In silence, we find our connection,
A silent oath, a pure affection.

Through trials faced, in every way,
Our silent devotion here to stay.
In every quiet, tender notion,
We live our silent, true devotion.

Spirit's Fondness

Beneath the canopy of ancient trees,
A whisper of the past, a gentle breeze,
In dances of the leaves, the spirit roams,
Finding solace in these verdant domes.

In twilight's tender glow, the heart unfolds,
A story of the times within it holds,
Each rustling leaf a testament, it seems,
To the spirit's fondness and its dreams.

With every step, the soul does intertwine,
With roots and branches, nature's grand design,
A journey through the forest, vast and deep,
Where memories of yesteryears do keep.

In silent reverie, the heart does sway,
To melodies the woodland spirits play,
A sanctuary where the mind finds ease,
Beneath the canopy of ancient trees.

Wellspring of Warmth

In mornings kissed by light, a tender touch,
A wellspring of warmth, it means so much,
Within the hearth, the embers softly glow,
A comfort only kindred hearts can know.

The sun's embrace, it paints a golden hue,
On fields of green, where flowers drink the dew,
The air is filled with whispers of the breeze,
A symphony of life among the trees.

In laughter shared beneath the azure skies,
A bond is formed where love and joy arise,
The warmth of friendship, like the morning sun,
That lights our days when darker hours come.

In quiet moments, tender and serene,
The wellspring of warmth is ever keen,
A beacon through the night, a steadfast flame,
Reminding us of love's enduring name.

Love's Undercurrent

Beneath the surface, deep and crystal clear,
An undercurrent strong, yet soft and near,
In every wave that laps upon the shore,
The echoes of a love forevermore.

In silent whispers carried by the tide,
The secrets of the heart cannot confide,
Yet in the moon's reflection on the sea,
Love's undercurrent sings in mystery.

Among the shells and stones the waters smooth,
A tale of timeless love their forms do soothe,
Each ripple writes the letters of a vow,
Invisible, yet sensed in here and now.

The ocean's depth, a mirror of the soul,
Where love's untamed and boundless waters roll,
In every breath of wind and salty spray,
Love's undercurrent flows both night and day.

Heartstrings and Horizons

Beyond the hills where twilight shadows fall,
A horizon beckons, calling one and all,
Where heartstrings pull and dreams begin to fly,
To realms where sun and moon share the sky.

In dawn's first light, the heart's aspirations soar,
To places unexplored, unknown before,
A journey marked by hopes and silent tears,
With heartstrings guiding through the fleeting years.

The vast expanse of sky, a canvas wide,
Where visions of tomorrow do reside,
Each heartbeat whispers tales of far-off lands,
And horizons drawn by fate's unseen hands.

In every end, a new beginning's trace,
Where heartstrings pull towards a broader space,
The horizon's edge, a promise yet to find,
A symphony of dreams in heart and mind.

Tender Tides

Beneath the moon's gentle glow,
Waves caress the shore so slow.
Whispers of the night unfold,
Secrets in the water bold.

Hearts adrift in ocean's song,
Where we both belong.
Tides of love that pull us near,
Erasing every trace of fear.

In this embrace of blue,
Promises remain true.
A world where dreams reside,
Caught within the tender tide.

The stars above reflect below,
Guiding where our hearts must go.
With every crest, a whispered rhyme,
A love that's endless, out of time.

Through dawn's first light, we'll stay,
Bound by night and break of day.
Forever in this dance we'll glide,
Together on the tender tide.

Labyrinth of Warmth

In a maze of golden light,
Paths of love are burning bright.
Whispers warm the coldest night,
Guiding steps with tender might.

Curves and turns with no end,
Where memories and feelings blend.
Heartbeats echo like a song,
In this labyrinth, we belong.

Soft eyes light the way,
Through the night into day.
Kindness flows like gentle streams,
Guardians of our hopes and dreams.

Bound by threads we cannot see,
Held in warmth, forever free.
In this maze where hearts reside,
Every shadow starts to hide.

From dawn till dusk, we're found,
In warmth's embrace, so profound.
Together we'll remain entwined,
In this labyrinth, souls aligned.

Wellspring of Kindness

From a source so deep and pure,
Flows a love that will endure.
Wellspring of a gentle heart,
Where kindness plays its endless part.

Every drop a precious gift,
Lives it touches start to lift.
In the softness of a sigh,
A spirit reaches, soaring high.

Ripples spread from every act,
Changing lives with tender tact.
In this wellspring, hope is found,
Where broken hearts become unbound.

With every gesture, grace is shown,
In words and deeds, our kindness grown.
A treasure trove of endless light,
Dispel the darkness of the night.

From this source, we drink deep,
Promises forever keep.
In the wellspring's loving flow,
Endless joy begins to grow.

Sanctuary of Feelings

Within these walls, emotions bloom,
A sanctuary free from gloom.
Where hearts can bare their tender soul,
And every feeling finds its role.

In shadows soft, and light so kind,
We leave our fears and doubts behind.
With every whisper, love takes flight,
In this sanctuary's gentle light.

Hopes and dreams are woven here,
In the silence, crystal clear.
Echoes of our deepest care,
In this refuge, hearts lay bare.

Comfort found in every gaze,
A peaceful, warm, embracing haze.
Here no tear or joy is small,
In this sanctuary, we find it all.

Wherever life may lead us next,
In this space, we're truly blessed.
A home of feelings, soft and true,
A sanctuary made for two.

Soulful Holdings

In quietude of dawn's gentle rise,
The soul awakens, opens eyes,
To whispers that the heart does keep,
In depths where silent dreams do sleep.

The holding hands of time extend,
Across the hours, hearts do blend,
Moments fleeting, yet so deep,
In sacred bonds, their secrets seep.

Alive in every heartbeat's song,
Where souls and spirits do belong,
A dance within, unseen, unknown,
In soulful holdings, love is shown.

Through night and day, the ties remain,
An unseen thread through joy and pain,
In silence, hearts will always meet,
In soulful holdings, pure and sweet.

Beneath the sky, where dreams ascend,
The human spirit finds its friend,
Embracing all with endless grace,
In soulful holdings, hearts embrace.

Heart's Gentle Harbinger

Upon the dawn of day's first light,
A tender whisper breaks the night,
A heartbeat soft, a message clear,
The harbinger of love draws near.

In glances shy, in quiet sighs,
The gentle herald never lies,
It brings to heart a soft embrace,
In moments fleeting, finds its place.

With every breath, the love grows true,
A bond unseen, yet felt by you,
A silent vow, a promise dear,
Heart's gentle harbinger is near.

In moonlit dreams, in realms of sleep,
The tender promise love will keep,
Through all of time, through all we fear,
Heart's gentle harbinger is here.

And in those eyes, where souls do meet,
A truth unfolds, so pure and sweet,
A constant flame, forever clear,
The heart's gentle harbinger sincere.

Gift of Tenderness

In the quiet of the morning dew,
A gift of tenderness anew,
Unwrapped in whispers, soft and kind,
A gentle touch, a mindful mind.

It graces life with silent ease,
A breath of warmth, a gentle breeze,
A treasure found in simple things,
In heart's own garden, softly sings.

Through trials faced and joys embraced,
In tender moments, love is traced,
In every smile and tear's caress,
We find the gift of tenderness.

With every word and tender glance,
In every shared, unspoken dance,
Love's purest gift, it softly flows,
In kindness, tender spirit grows.

So hold this gift, so gentle, true,
Within your heart, it lives in you,
A timeless bond, a gentle theme,
The gift of tenderness, supreme.

Embrace of the Soul

In twilight's hues, where dreams collide,
An unseen force does gently guide,
The weary heart and wanderer whole,
Find solace in the soul's embrace.

It spans across the vast unknown,
In whispering winds, the seeds are sown,
A comfort deep, a resting grace,
In the embrace of the soul's place.

Through trials vast and moments brief,
The soul provides its sweet relief,
A hug unseen, a warm, soft light,
To guide us through the darkest night.

With every breath, with every beat,
The soul's embrace, a refuge sweet,
A timeless bond, a sacred space,
In every heart, its tender trace.

So listen close, in stillness find,
The soul's embrace, a love so kind,
It holds us true, through all we face,
In timeless, pure, and gentle grace.

Boundless Grace

In fields where lilies waltz and sway,
A whisper of grace fills the air,
Stars paint stories, night and day,
In blessings breathed through gentle care.

Time's endless river flows serene,
With every heart's forgiving trace,
A spectrum of the unseen,
In realms of boundless, perfect grace.

Songs of hope on wings do fly,
As dawn's first light begins to trace,
The tear-streaked faces lifted high,
In gratitude for boundless grace.

Embrace the dreams that softly speak,
Of kindness in the human race,
A strength found hidden in the weak,
The beauty of a boundless grace.

Bright eyes break through clouds of gray,
Hearts unified in this embrace,
In fleeting moments, come what may,
We find solace in boundless grace.

River of Embrace

Calm whispers flow through winding streams,
A river's song in soft embrace,
Uniting us beneath moonbeams,
In tranquil paths of liquid grace.

Mountains bow to kiss the shore,
Where waters dance with gentle trace,
Echoes of love forevermore,
In the river's warm embrace.

Shadows flee as dawn arrives,
Painting skies with hues of lace,
Morning wakes and love revives,
Carried by the river's embrace.

Silence speaks in rhythmic waves,
Hopes and dreams in liquid maze,
Unity that boundless saves,
Guided by the river's embrace.

Flowing endlessly through time,
Whispers soft of love's own base,
Connecting hearts in every clime,
An eternal river's embrace.

Portrait of Passion

A canvas stretched through time and space,
Colors blend in love's grand frame,
Each brushstroke fierce in its embrace,
A portrait bound by passion's flame.

Eyes that shine with fire's light,
Lips that speak in hushed acclaim,
Silhouettes in shadowed night,
In the portrait of passion's name.

Hearts beat wild in synced embrace,
A rhythm built within this game,
Two souls caught in timeless chase,
In the portrait of passion's flame.

Every line tells tales untold,
Of days when fire and storm both came,
Scenes of love both free and bold,
Etched in portrait's passionate fame.

A masterpiece of flames that rise,
Under moon's soft glowing claim,
Art that lives in lovers' eyes,
In their portrait of passion's flame.

Beacons of Compassion

On stormy seas, where shadows hide,
A guiding light does softly gleam,
Through darkness that the world defied,
Compassion's beacon, constant beam.

An uncharted path through night,
Hearts that heal with tender scheme,
In every soul, a shining light,
A beacon of compassion's dream.

As stars align in cosmic grace,
Love does weave with gentle seam,
In every kind and caring face,
The beacon's glow, a steady stream.

Through trials that the soul may face,
Hope survives in warmest theme,
Lighthouse beamed in love's embrace,
Compassion's beacon lights the dream.

United, we stand in gentle flame,
Guided by this radiant gleam,
Through every hardship, one and same,
Beacons of compassion beam.

Compassionate Currents

In waters deep, where shadows play,
A gentle heart sends waves anew,
With each kind act, the dawning day,
Transforms the dark to pastel hues.

The ripples cast by careful hands,
Extend beyond the eyes can see,
And so they weave compassion's bands,
Across the depths of boundless sea.

Beneath the surface, silent song,
Of empathy and soft embrace,
A current pure, unwavering, strong,
To touch, to heal, to interlace.

In every droplet's tender kiss,
A world awakes to gracious light,
Where loving kindness finds its bliss,
And dawn becomes the endless night.

These currents move, forever kind,
Binding hearts with threads unseen,
An ocean of the gentle mind,
Where every soul can rest serene.

Internal Glow

In quiet moments, soft and still,
A spark ignites, a gentle flame,
Within the heart, against the chill,
A beacon known by no one's name.

It dances there with fervent grace,
Through shadowed thoughts, it weaves and winds,
Illuminates each hidden space,
A warmth the searching spirit finds.

Its glow reflects in mindful eyes,
A mirror to the soul's deep core,
Embracing truth, no dark disguise,
Inviting light to love what's more.

Through trials faced and paths unknown,
This inner fire, it never wanes,
It guides through fears, to strength alone,
Where courage in the heart remains.

So tend this glow with tender care,
For it's the light within the mind,
A flame that lives, eternally fair,
In every soul so intertwined.

Overflowing Emotions

A heart awash in colors bright,
With every beat, emotions rise,
Each tide of feeling taking flight,
A storm within, a paradise.

The joy that sweeps on wings of cheer,
Unfurls its banner bold and high,
While sorrow's rain can bring so near,
The memories that softly sigh.

In laughter's echo, pure delight,
A melody of heart's sweet release,
And in the tears of midnight bright,
A serenade of tender peace.

These waves of love, of hope, of grief,
They carve the shores of time and space,
Each moment's touch, so bright, so brief,
A trace of life's dear, gentle grace.

O let them flow, these currents deep,
For in their course, a soul's reborn,
In every passion, wake or sleep,
The fabric of a heart is worn.

The Essence of Care

In every touch, a story told,
Of love's intent, so pure, so rare,
In whispers soft, in gestures bold,
There lies the essence of true care.

A gentle hand to soothe the pain,
A tender word to ease the mind,
Compassion's glow, like summer rain,
To nourish hearts, to stand aligned.

Through trials faced and hopes once lost,
This beacon shines, unwavering,
It mends the soul at any cost,
With every act, love savouring.

In kindness given, light is sown,
A radiant warmth that never parts,
It grows within, its presence known,
In bonds of love and open hearts.

So cherish well each caring deed,
For in its wake, the world can heal,
With every heart that's ever freed,
By hands that care and truly feel.

Whispers of the Heart

In the still of night, they start,
Barely audible, yet grand,
Echoes from a mystic part,
A language only hearts understand.

Through the hush, they softly sing,
Dreams and fears they do impart,
Secrets on a fragile wing,
Whispers from a tender heart.

In the silence, they confide,
Wishes woven, wrapped in art,
Mysteries where love resides,
In whispers of the quiet heart.

They dance upon the twilight air,
Invisible, yet sharps the dart,
Binding souls beyond compare,
In whispers, where true loves start.

Silhouette of Dedication

Underneath the morning sky,
In the quiet, breaking dawn,
Silhouettes begin to try,
Crafting futures till they're gone.

Every stroke is laced with care,
Patience shadowed by their form,
Dedication fills the air,
Silent pledge to weather storms.

Through the toils, they never rest,
Eyes on goals, they stay aligned,
In each heart, a fervent quest,
Duty's fire, brightly shined.

Shadows lengthen, deeds endure,
Faces marked by time's own hand,
In silhouettes so pure,
Stands dedication's solemn band.

Chorus of Kindness

In a world that seems so vast,
Kindness weaves a tender thread,
Moments shared, then quickly passed,
In the heart, their echoes spread.

Gentle words and softly spoken,
Acts that heal, hands that mend,
In these bonds, no promise broken,
Kindness speaks with love, its friend.

Every smile, a precious note,
In a chorus, sweet and clear,
Ripples loud, wild dreams it dotes,
Amid the silence, you'll then hear.

For in each, a part is sung,
In every heart, this truth we've won,
Through the strife, we're all among,
A chorus of kindness, never done.

Embers of Affection

When the night draws still and deep,
In the quiet, embers glow,
Lingering warmth that shadows keep,
Affection's quiet, tender show.

In those sparks, a story told,
Silent whispers, golden hue,
Tales of love, both shy and bold,
In embers, love's light anew.

Through the cold, they softly shine,
Burning bright with memories,
In their glow, our hearts realign,
Bound by unseen tender ties.

For as long as embers gleam,
Affection's flame will never die,
Holding fast to every dream,
In fires love, we'll always fly.

Path of Benevolence

In the silence of the dawn,
Where the gentle breezes sing,
Lies a road that leads us on,
To the warmth of everything.

Step by step with hearts anew,
Hand in hand we walk as one,
Kindness forms a sacred cue,
Underneath the steadfast sun.

On this path of giving light,
Every shadow finds its way,
Compassion binds firm and tight,
Guiding each and every day.

Here, no tear shall be in vain,
For we turn strife into grace,
Empathy our guiding chain,
Illuminates each face.

With each act of love, we grow,
Paths of benevolence we pave,
In each heart, a brighter glow,
With kindness, we are brave.

Wings of Warmth

On wings of warmth, we rise above,
The bitter cold and cruel of night,
In the arms of endless love,
Hearts take flight to realms of light.

Gently whisper through the air,
Songs of comfort, soft and mild,
Cradle all that's pure and fair,
Like a mother's soothing child.

Each tender word and loving glance,
Turns the darkest days to gold,
In this gentle, sacred dance,
Breathes the warmth of tales untold.

Through the storms and through the tide,
Hold each other, firm, and strong,
In love's shelter we confide,
Wings of warmth will bring us home.

Find the beauty in the calm,
In the quiet, hear love's call,
Wrap the world in tender balm,
On wings of warmth, we heal all.

Veil of Tenderness

Beneath a veil of tenderness,
Gentle whispers softly stream,
Caressing hearts with mild finesse,
In the sanctuary of a dream.

Eyes that meet and hands that touch,
Stories woven, souls entwined,
In this love that means so much,
Lives and fates so sweetly designed.

Underneath this tranquil veil,
Wounds of old begin to mend,
Every sigh and every tale,
Merging glances that transcend.

Breathe the softness, taste the trust,
Tender moments linger, sweet,
From the ashes to the dust,
In tenderness, our spirits meet.

Hold this gentle, sacred weave,
In the fabric of our time,
Through the veil, our hearts receive,
Endless love so pure, divine.

Starlit Affection

In the hush of twilight's reign,
Starlit affection softly blooms,
Woven in each gentle chain,
Hearts alight in evening's rooms.

Glance skyward and feel the grace,
Glimmered whispers in the night,
Luminescence on each face,
Bound by love's enduring light.

Through the constellations' glow,
Dreams are whispered, sweet and clear,
Guiding where true hearts can go,
In the cosmos, souls draw near.

In each twinkle, find a vow,
Promises that softly gleam,
Radiant love in night's silent bow,
In its glow, forever dream.

Love's celestial, gentle kiss,
Under starlit skies we sway,
Wrapped in pure, unending bliss,
Hearts the night shall never sway.

Harbor of Feelings

In the gentle harbor where feelings rest,
Whispers of the sea are put to test,
Waves of time come crashing bright,
In the heart's embrace, it's always night.

Moody skies paint shades of blue,
Reflections of the dreams we pursue,
Anchored by hopes both old and new,
In the harbor, love remains true.

Stars above guide the silent tides,
Ebbing softly, where everything hides,
Breezes carry secrets untold,
In this harbor, we are bold.

Lighthouses of trust shine their beam,
Illuminating every tender dream,
Within this harbor, hearts intertwine,
Timeless love is the sweetest wine.

In the calm of this gentle space,
Feelings find their rightful place,
Resting safe from distant storms,
In the harbor, all hearts are warm.

Vessel of Emotion

A vessel sails on a sea so wide,
Carrying emotions deep inside,
Each wave a whisper, each breeze a sigh,
Across the waters, dreams do fly.

Upon this journey, hearts do ride,
Navigating the ocean's tide,
The sails are woven with every tear,
Guiding love both far and near.

Storms may rage and winds may cry,
Onward sails with spirits high,
In the vessel, emotions climb,
Riding through the waves of time.

Anchored moments linger long,
Singing a bittersweet song,
Every emotion etched in the mast,
In the vessel, shadows are cast.

When the dawn breaks, soft and light,
Feelings emerge in the early twilight,
In the vessel, pure devotion,
Across the endless, boundless ocean.

Cradle of Care

In the cradle where care is sown,
Tenderness and love are grown,
Lullabies in whispers find,
A soothing peace, a gentle mind.

Rocking softly in embrace,
Cradle of care, a sacred place,
Hearts entwined in woven grace,
Where worries vanish without trace.

Underneath the stars' bright gleam,
Nurtured dreams like soft moonbeam,
In the cradle, safe and warm,
Love's true essence takes its form.

Softly spoken words imbue,
Promises that all hold true,
Careful hands and hearts align,
In this cradle, care divine.

As the night gives way to dawn,
Care continues, ever drawn,
In the cradle, love and trust,
Carry forth, gentle and just.

Guardian of Warmth

In the heart's core, a guardian stands,
Protecting warmth with gentle hands,
A flicker of flame, love's tender light,
Illuminates the darkest night.

Guardian keeps the fire's glow,
In every heart where embers show,
With whispers soft, the warmth remains,
Banishing life's cold, bitter chains.

In moments frail, the warmth does spread,
Comforting, where fears have led,
A shield of hope, a light so soft,
Keeping hearts securely aloft.

The guardian stands through storm and rain,
Bearing love, warding off pain,
In the warmth's eternal embrace,
Every heart finds its grace.

When shadows fall and strength does wane,
Guardian brings warmth again,
In this hearth, love's glow does lie,
Tender, true, it will never die.

Mosaic of Feelings

Fragments of joy in the morning light,
Tears that shimmer in the night.
Threads of hope, woven tight,
In the quilt of dreams so bright.

Laughter echoes through the halls,
Whispers pass through ancient walls.
Painted hearts where love installs,
A mosaic where emotion calls.

Anguish fades in shadows deep,
Secrets that we vow to keep.
Memories in minds that sleep,
A treasure chest that's lost in heaps.

Waves of sorrow on the shore,
Stories that we can't ignore.
In the silence, craving more,
A mosaic of what came before.

Hands that touch, yet yearn to feel,
Moments that we can't conceal.
In time's embrace, wounds to heal,
The mosaic shows what's real.

Ether of Affection

Whispers in the evening mist,
Lips that memory couldn't resist.
A fleeting touch, a gentle twist,
In the ether, love's enlist.

Stars that sparkle in the night,
Feelings that take sudden flight.
In moments pure, and hearts so light,
Affection's glow, a tender sight.

Souls that meet beyond the veil,
Love's soft whispers, never frail.
In the ether, we set sail,
A journey where affection prevails.

Eyes that speak without a word,
In silence, passions undeterred.
Affection's flight, like a bird,
In the ether, deeply heard.

Hands that reach, but never touch,
In this ether, love is much.
With every glance, with every clutch,
Affection lives in hearts' very hush.

Gentle Lighthouses

Beacons in the stormy night,
Guiding ships with steady light.
Through the fog, in darkest plight,
Lighthouses stand in might.

Stories told by ancient towers,
Holding hope through endless hours.
Guiding lost in trying showers,
Gentle strength their light empowers.

Waves crashing on the shore,
Lighthouses guide evermore.
Silent sentinels, hearts implore,
In their glow, we find the core.

Eyes that search the dark unknown,
Hearts that long to be homegrown.
In their light, we're not alone,
Gentle lighthouses, brightly shone.

Among the stars and ocean's roar,
They stand tall along the shore.
With their light, our spirits soar,
Gentle lighthouses, forevermore.

Infinitesimal Tenderness

In the quiet, whispers grow,
Tiny seeds in soft winds blow.
Heartfelt warmth in gentle flow,
Tender moments, love bestows.

Eyes that soften, hearts align,
Hands that touch in perfect time.
With each glance, a love divine,
Infinitesimal, yet it shines.

Moments small, yet deeply grand,
In these touches, understand.
Life's great weave in willful strands,
Tenderness in every hand.

Tiny gestures, meaning vast,
Love's sweet echo from the past.
In each instant, make it last,
Infinitesimal, yet steadfast.

Beneath the stars, and in between,
Tenderness in night's serene.
In small acts, our spirits glean,
Love infinitesimal, yet keen.

Profound Connections

In silent heartbeats, whispers flow,
Through veins of time, where moments grow,
A touch unseen, yet deeply felt,
In bonds unspoken, we have knelt.

Eyes that meet in cosmic dance,
Familiar glances, a fleeting chance,
Threads of fate, so finely spun,
Weaving lives, until they're one.

Unseen but known, these ties profound,
In quiet whispers, love is found,
A soul's embrace, a gentle hand,
Traveling realms where dreams command.

Though miles apart may stretch the land,
In kindred spirits, we still stand,
Together in this vast expanse,
Beyond mere sight, in love's grand stance.

With every breath, a silent note,
In harmony, our spirits float,
Invisible, unbreakable threads,
Connecting hearts across life's spreads.

Shadows of Warmth

Beneath the moon's soft, tender glow,
In shadows cast, our secrets grow,
Warmth hidden in the cool night air,
A silent vow, a whispered prayer.

The stars, they twinkle, soft and bright,
Guiding us through the velvet night,
A shadow here, a shadow there,
In every shade, love's constant care.

In absence, presence softly hums,
The warmth of touch in darkness comes,
An unseen flame, forever burns,
Against cold night, the heart yearns.

Whispers ride on twilight's breeze,
Promise linger in night's embrace,
Shadows paint a kind caress,
In stillness, warmth we confess.

Through the darkness, through the night,
Love's shadow casts eternal light,
In every corner, every bend,
A warmth that only hearts defend.

Binding Hearts

Two souls entwined in dance so fine,
In love's embrace, our hearts align,
A binding thread, unseen yet fierce,
Together strong, each wound it pierces.

In every heartbeat, you are near,
A melody both bright and clear,
A harmony in time we share,
In moments light, in burdens bare.

Through trials faced and joys we find,
Our spirits grow, our hearts combined,
A sacred vow, a precious trust,
In binding hearts, love's arms we thrust.

The ties that weave us, soft yet strong,
In love's domain, we both belong,
With every breath, each whispered word,
Our hearts in tandem softly heard.

Though life may bring its twists and turns,
The flame of love within us burns,
In binding hearts, we find our way,
Together strong, come night or day.

Breath of Compassion

In gentlest breeze, compassion lives,
A breath that each of us forgives,
Soft whispers in the silent air,
A tender touch, a loving care.

Eyes that see beyond the veil,
To hearts that ache, and souls that wail,
A kindness wrapped in soft embrace,
With every breath, a gentle grace.

The world may spin its hurried dance,
But in compassion, we enhance,
A moment's pause, a hand to hold,
In empathy, our hearts unfold.

With every sigh, a story shared,
In love's own language, hearts repaired,
A breath of warmth in coldest night,
In compassion, we share the light.

So let us breathe in unison,
A world of love, of hearts begun,
For in each breath, compassion flows,
A life's purpose, the heart bestows.

Intangible Bonds

Invisible threads that deftly twine,
Connecting hearts through space and time.
Silent whispers in the dark,
A spark ignites, a lasting mark.

Beneath the stars, we find our path,
No need for words, no aftermath.
A glance exchanged, a touch unseen,
In this world, we softly dream.

Bound by more than what we see,
A deeper truth, our mystery.
These ties of soul, forever free,
In quiet moments, you're with me.

A bond that distance can't erase,
A love that time cannot displace.
Through trials faced and joys embraced,
In our hearts, we find our place.

Intangible, yet oh so real,
This force we sense, this bond we feel.
Beyond the realm of mere ideal,
Our souls, united, seal the deal.

The Substance of Grace

In gentle whispers, grace is found,
A quiet strength, without a sound.
It lifts us when we're feeling small,
A hand to catch us when we fall.

In every gesture, pure and kind,
A touch that heals, a hand that binds.
The essence of the peaceful heart,
The light that guides us from the start.

In moments fleeting, grace appears,
To wipe away our doubt and fears.
A silent calm, a tranquil sea,
Reflecting all that we can be.

Through trials faced and battles fought,
With grace, each lesson is then taught.
The humble soul, the kindly deed,
From these, the heart can learn to lead.

The substance of this noble art,
Inspires warmth in every heart.
A gentle power, soft and fierce,
A love that time cannot pierce.

Layers of Devotion

In layers deep, devotion lies,
Veiled beneath the worldly guise.
With every act of love displayed,
A silent promise, softly made.

Through trials that the heart endures,
Devotion's essence reassures.
A steadfast bond that won't decline,
A gentle force, so pure, divine.

Each sacrifice, so freely given,
A step towards the life we're driven.
In every moment, love unfolds,
A tale of warmth and care retold.

When darkness falls and shadows creep,
Devotion's light, our path will keep.
In layers thick, through night and day,
Its presence guides, come what may.

A love profound, in layers deep,
A silent vow, forever keep.
Through storm and sun, in heart's pure notion,
Abiding trust, in pure devotion.

Echoing Kindness

Kind words like echoes softly ring,
They touch the heart, they gently sing.
Through every deed that's kindly done,
A ripple set, in unison.

In acts so small, the heart reveals,
A strength in kindness, gently heals.
Each echo carried through the air,
A whisper of, 'I see, I care.'

Compassion flows in every touch,
A kindness given means so much.
From soul to soul, the echo flies,
A simple truth that never dies.

When life is harsh and days are long,
Kindness sings a soothing song.
In echoes of the heart's embrace,
We find our light, we find our place.

So let your kindness echo wide,
In every heart, let it abide.
As echoes join and kindness grows,
The world, a garden, gently sows.

Harmony of Empathy

In quiet whispers, hearts unfold,
With gentle words, compassion sold.
A tender hand extends its grace,
In shared warmth, we find our place.

Through tear-filled eyes, we see anew,
In every soul, a world in view.
United paths, together strong,
In empathy, where we belong.

With every touch, a story told,
In kindness, courage we uphold.
A symphony of minds and hearts,
In harmony, our journey starts.

No bounds to break, no walls to mend,
In love and trust, we comprehend.
A world where care and hope combine,
In every heart, the stars align.

Through shadows cast, we light the way,
In empathy, we learn to say,
We'll stand as one, forever free,
In harmony, humanity.

Veins of Tenderness

Through veins of tenderness, love flows,
In silent streams, it gently grows.
A touch, a glance, a soft caress,
Moments woven, a quiet bless.

In the tapestry of hearts entwined,
Unseen rivers, softly aligned.
Whispers breathe in the night's stillness,
Through veins of tender, pure finesse.

Heartbeat Symphony

In rhythmic waves, our pulses beat,
A symphony, where hearts compete.
A dance of life, in time aligned,
In every note, connection find.

Beneath the sky, with stars above,
We weave a tale of endless love.
With every breath, we forge a song,
In heartbeat, where we all belong.

With each crescendo, passion grows,
In every chord, emotion flows.
A melody of hope and light,
In chorus, darkness takes its flight.

United hearts, in harmony,
Compose a timeless symphony.
A cadence pure, a rhythm true,
In every beat, we find the glue.

For love and life, a dance divine,
In heartbeat's song, we intertwine.
A symphony for all to hear,
In every heart, it echoes clear.

Gentle Waves of Care

On shores of life, with tender crest,
The waves of care, in hearts invest.
A soothing balm, in flowing tide,
In gentle waves, our fears subside.

Through storms and squalls, we find our peace,
In loving hands, our doubts release.
With every wave, a promise sent,
In care's embrace, our hearts relent.

The ocean's breath, a sweet caress,
In every touch, a soft finesse.
A rhythmic dance, in ebb and flow,
In waves of care, our spirits grow.

Beneath the moon's serene embrace,
In steady tides, we find our place.
A tranquil dream, in waters deep,
In every wave, our souls to keep.

So let us drift, on caring seas,
In tender waves, a sense of ease.
Unite in warmth, forever share,
In gentle waves, we show we care.

Orchestra of Embrace

In arms outstretched, a warm embrace,
A symphony in shared space.
With tender notes and heartfelt ties,
In loving arms, our spirits rise.

A dance of bonds, in sweet refrain,
In every hug, we break the chain.
With whispered vows and gentle key,
In clutching holds, we find we're free.

From heart to heart, a melody,
In every touch, our symphony.
An orchestra, of love composed,
In close embrace, our fears deposed.

A concert grand, of human kind,
In every chord, a soul aligned.
Through joy and pain, we share the beat,
In loving arms, our worlds complete.

So may we play this song of care,
In every hug, our hearts lay bare.
An orchestra, in love's embrace,
In every heart, we find our place.

Warmth in the Silence

Silent whispers in the night
Hold me close within their might
Soft and tender, warmly fuse
Mornings bathed in golden hues

In the quiet, hearts converse
Gentle songs of the universe
Kindred spirits, side by side
Serenade the ebbing tide

Hushed embraces, soothing balm
Echoing a healing calm
Teach me all the stars confess
Silence woven, pure duress

Unspoken vows, deep and true
Wrapped in twilight's softest blue
Every breath a silent prayer
In the stillness, love lays bare

Warmth abounds in hushed repose
Silent bond that ever grows
Hold my heart with gentle grace
Filled with love in silence's space

The Capacity to Adore

Within my soul, a wellspring pure
Endless love I know for sure
In the depth of heart's great store
Flows the capacity to adore

Sunrise kisses morning dew
Angles bathed in golden hue
Every moment, something more
In the capacity to adore

Eyes connect and sparks ignite
Underneath the silvered night
From the core, emotions pour
With the capacity to adore

Truth and mercy intertwined
Gentle hands and hearts aligned
In this bond, we will explore
The capacity to adore

Hand in hand, we'll always be
Bound by love eternally
In our hearts, a boundless door
To the capacity to adore

Ingrained Affections

In grains of sand, love's deeply sown
Affections ingrained, brightly shone
Each embrace, a timeless art
Gently sculpted, heart by heart

Ancient roots intertwine below
Tendrils of affection grow
Years may pass, yet still they stand
Love and time, they walk hand in hand

Crafted by the hands of fate
Affections ingrained, love create
Moments etched in heart and mind
Union formed, a bond refined

Waves may crash, and storms may roar
Yet our love endures the more
Seasons fade, but we remain
Affections ingrained through joy and pain

In our souls, the story stays
Paths diverge, yet hearts don't stray
Carved in truth, forever more
Ingrained affections we adore

Veins of Compassion

Like rivers flowing, hearts expand
Through veins of compassion, hand in hand
Each beat a testament to grace
Bridging gaps in time and space

With every act, a seed is sown
Love's compassion brightly shown
In moments frail, we find our strength
Stretching mercy's boundless length

Healing words and tender touch
Veins of compassion mean so much
In life's grand tapestry we weave
Threads of care as we believe

To heal the world, to mend a heart
Compassion's vein in every part
A simple smile, a gentle word
In this, our kindness is unblurred

Through veins of compassion, hearts conflate
Creating bonds we celebrate
Limitless, the love we show
In these veins, compassion flows

Ember Glow

In the heart of night, an ember glows,
Softly whispering ancient prose.
Stars above, like scattered pearls,
Dance in rhythm, their stories unfurled.

Shadows flicker, the fire's embrace,
Silent secrets held in space.
Timeless echoes, whispers low,
In the heart of night, an ember glows.

River of Warmth

Beneath the winter's icy crown,
A river of warmth flows deep down.
Carving paths where shadows lie,
In hidden veins, life will not die.

Sunlight trickles through the snow,
A promise kept, a subtle glow.
In the heart where frost may cling,
Flows a river, forever spring.

Compass of Compassion

In the realm of doubt and fear,
A compass of compassion steers.
Guiding hearts through stormy seas,
To shores of kindness, gentle breeze.

With steady hand and open heart,
Navigating where shadows start.
In the darkest, deepest night,
Compassion's compass leads to light.

The Resonance of Affection

Whispers of love on a gentle breeze,
In the twilight's softest tone,
Resonate through the hearts at ease,
A melody that's all our own.

In the hush of evening's song,
Affection weaves an endless thread,
A bond both tender and strong,
In the silent words unsaid.

Eyes that speak without a sound,
Hands that meet with gentle care,
Love in every look is found,
In the moments we both share.

Stars above bear witness true,
To the symphony we create,
In every heartbeat, always new,
A love that time cannot abate.

Through the years, like waves on sand,
Our resonance will softly grow,
With each touch, and with each hand,
The depths of our affection show.

A Symphony of Feelings

In dawn's first light, emotions rise,
A symphony begins anew,
In our hearts, a paradise,
In colors bright and true.

Harmonies that softly blend,
In each smile and tender glance,
Love's melody will never end,
A timeless, sweet romance.

Chords of passion, notes of grace,
Entwine our souls as one,
In your arms, a sacred place,
Where love will never be undone.

Verses sung in evening's gold,
Resonate through twilight's grays,
In our hearts, a story told,
In love's enduring embrace.

Echoes of our laughter dance,
Through the air, the night, the day,
In this symphony of chance,
Our feelings find their way.

Innate Tenderness

In the quiet of the morn,
Where sunlight gently gleams,
Tenderness is softly born,
In the realm of dreams.

Eyes that touch with gentle care,
Speak of love in silent ways,
In every whispered prayer,
In nights and in days.

A touch that heals, a heart that knows,
The purest form of what is true,
In every gentle wind that blows,
Tenderness is what we pursue.

Within the depths of every soul,
Lies a seed of care profound,
In our love, we are made whole,
In each moment that we've found.

In the kindness we unfurl,
In the hearts we softly mend,
Tenderness will shape the world,
In this love that has no end.

Heart's Heirlooms

Memories that softly glow,
In the heart's most secret place,
Treasures that the years bestow,
In love's eternal grace.

Whispered words in twilight's hue,
Moments frozen in sweet time,
In each heartbeat echoing true,
In a gentle rhythm, rhyme.

Photographs of smiles shared,
Laughter in the golden light,
Every tear and joy that bared,
In the heart, forever bright.

Stories told and dreams revealed,
In the warmth of tender care,
In our hearts forever sealed,
Love's heirlooms beyond compare.

In the tapestry we weave,
With threads of purest gold,
Heart's heirlooms we receive,
In every lifetime's fold.

Radiance of Affection

In twilight's soft and tender glow,
Our hearts to one another show,
Whispered words in moonlight's sheen,
Bind the spirits, pure and keen.

Hands entwined, we softly tread,
Through the thoughts and dreams we've said,
A dance of souls beneath the sky,
In love's embrace, we'll ever lie.

The stars above, they shimmer bright,
Casting hues in velvet night,
A union warm, a bond so tight,
In every dawn, in every light.

With every touch, a vibrant spark,
They guide us through the night's own dark,
A beacon through the deepest shade,
In softest breaths, affection laid.

Together we forge a glowing path,
In sun and moon, an endless bath,
In joys of life, our hearts in flight,
Affection's radiance, pure delight.

Sea of Serenity

Beneath the azure, skies so wide,
Where waves and earth in peace abide,
A silent call, a tranquil plea,
In this embrace of tranquil sea.

The whispers of the ocean's song,
Gently guide our hearts along,
In gentle rhythms, soft and free,
We find our calm, our sanctuary.

On sands that drift with time's own hand,
We wander through this endless land,
With every step, with every tide,
Our worries from our minds now slide.

The moon's sweet glow, a guiding light,
Through every storm, through every night,
In salt-kissed winds, we find our truth,
A timeless peace, eternal youth.

In the sea's embrace, so endlessly,
We touch the soul of serenity,
A dance of waves, a song so sweet,
In ocean's arms, our spirits meet.

Field of Devotion

In fields where golden sunsets gleam,
We walk as one, within a dream,
With every step, with every mile,
Devotion's path, our hearts compile.

Through meadows vast where wildflowers grow,
A bond that's built in gentle slow,
In every bloom, in every sigh,
Our hearts aligned beneath the sky.

The whispers of the wind declare,
A love that's pure, beyond compare,
In sunlit beams and moonlit eves,
Our spirits sow what love believes.

With hands entwined, we weave our tale,
Through every storm, through calm and gale,
A promise held, a vow so true,
In fields of gold, where love renews.

Together we'll remain as one,
Until the stars no longer run,
In fields of devotion, life interweaves,
A tapestry of hearts that never leaves.

Mirrors of the Heart

In mirrors of the heart, we see,
Reflections pure and sanctuary,
With every glance, a tale unfolds,
A love that's vast and yet untold.

The eyes that gaze with understanding,
See beyond the walls so demanding,
In silent glimpses, truths impart,
The echoes of a beating heart.

Each pulse a rhythm, each beat a prayer,
In mirrored souls beyond compare,
A union rare where hearts align,
In tender glances, love defines.

Through mirrors bright, our fears dissolve,
In unity, our souls evolve,
With every look, with every start,
We map the contours of the heart.

In every mirrored glance we share,
A love that shows us how to care,
In heartbeats pure and souls so clear,
Our love reflects eternal here.

Whispers of Affection

In twilight's gentle embrace,
Lovers find their secret place.
Silent words the heart does send,
Unheard whispers never end.

Stars above begin to gleam,
Lit by love's eternal dream.
Murmured secrets softly flow,
In affection's tender glow.

Hands entwined with sweetest grace,
Time, it halts in this embrace.
Each caress, a silent word,
Of affection gently stirred.

Eyes that speak in silent rhyme,
Mark the passage of their time.
Each soft look, a pledge anew,
In the night, their love holds true.

Through the years and through the tears,
Love remains, despite the fears.
Whispered words of deep affection,
Echo on, in their connection.

Moonlit Serenade

Beneath the moon's ethereal light,
Soft melodies fill the night.
Crickets sing a lullaby,
Stars are twinkling in the sky.

Though the world is deep in sleep,
Lovers' hearts a vigil keep.
Whispers in the night they trade,
This their moonlit serenade.

Shadows dance upon the grass,
Marking moments as they pass.
Softly sung, the love's refrain,
Eclipsing all earthly pain.

Moonbeams cast a tender glow,
Silhouettes in love's tableau.
In this tranquil, silent glade,
Plays the moonlit serenade.

Promises in whispers made,
Underneath this night's facade.
Endless as the celestial bands,
Bound by moonlight's gentle hands.

Unseen Caress

A touch like whispers in the breeze,
Invisible, yet aims to please.
Fingertips, they softly trace,
Unseen caresses in this space.

Through the night, the shadows glide,
Hands of love, they never hide.
Feeling warmth in every breath,
Unseen caress defying death.

Moments held in tender bonds,
Echoes in our heart responds.
Silent lips that part to kiss,
Unseen caress, a timeless bliss.

In the silence of the night,
Feelings rise to take the flight.
In the heart, the souls confess,
To an unseen, soft caress.

Love that's felt but never seen,
Like a touch within a dream.
Gentle as the morning's light,
Unseen caress, pure delight.

Veins of Devotion

Through the veins, love's course does run,
Bound by heartbeats, one by one.
In the silence, in the throng,
Devotion's melody, a song.

Every pulse a pledge it makes,
Every beat, where love awakes.
Threads of passion intertwine,
In devotion's grand design.

Feel the warmth beneath the skin,
Where the truest love begins.
Life and love, a fusion fine,
In these veins, they both entwine.

Time and trials, they may test,
This devotion in our chest.
Stronger grows with every tide,
In the hearts where love resides.

Bound by flow and bound by fate,
Love within will never abate.
In these veins of deep devotion,
Flows a love of pure emotion.

Eternal Sympathies

In twilight's gentle, whispered grace,
The stars emerge, a soft embrace.
Mournful tunes in shadows play,
Eternal sympathies, they say.

A heart once broken, now will mend,
With time, the soul learns to defend.
Through night's embrace, we find anew,
The strength within, the hope anew.

Memories like autumn leaves,
Dance in twilight, as night weaves.
Sympathies in stars, they glisten,
To the heart's deep plea, they listen.

Journey through the darkened skies,
Seek the truth in sorrow's eyes.
Feel the warmth of unseen ties,
In each heart, a soul's sunrise.

Boundless as the evening sea,
In whispers soft, eternally.
Sympathetic notes, they ring,
In a timeless, soft, kind spring.

Hidden Embraces

In moonlit meadows, shadows lie,
Secrets held beneath the sky.
With delicate and tender trace,
Hidden lies each soft embrace.

A whisper through the willow's sigh,
Promises that never die.
In the hush of midnight's race,
Feel the hidden, soft embrace.

Veil of night and starry glow,
Love in secret takes its flow.
In the quiet, stolen space,
Breathes the hidden, warm embrace.

Rustling leaves and gentle breeze,
Silent vows beneath the trees.
Wrapped in love's most sacred lace,
Cherishing the hidden embrace.

Mysterious as moon's soft gleam,
Fleeting like a tender dream.
In the night's sweet, silent grace,
Exists the hidden, gentle embrace.

Unspoken Tenderness

Eyes that meet in silent gaze,
Hearts that beat in gentle phase.
Unseen threads that bind and weave,
Unspoken words softly cleave.

A touch that lingers, soft and light,
In the quiet of the night.
Tenderness in silence speaks,
In the moments, love it seeks.

Through the whisper of a sigh,
In the tear that leaves an eye.
Silent words of deep caress,
Speak of love's unspoken press.

Gentle as the morning dew,
Hidden feelings, strong yet true.
In a world where words digress,
Lives the pure, unspoken press.

Bonds that form in quietness,
Strong and true, a sweet finesse.
In the calm of love's recess,
Whispers love, unspoken press.

The Soul's Caress

In the silence of the night,
Where the stars are glowing bright.
Feel the touch, the soul's caress,
In the night's soft, sweet finesse.

Gentle as a feather's fall,
Whispers in the shadows call.
In the calm, the heart's recess,
Lives the soul's most tender press.

Dreams that dance on starlit beams,
Fill the night with gentle gleams.
Softly through the void, they bless,
With a tender, soul's caress.

In each quiet, tender space,
Feel the love's most soft embrace.
Through the night, its sweet caress,
Soothes the heart, the soul's press.

Timeless as the moon's soft gleam,
In the quiet, heart's sweet dream.
Feel the night's soft, sweet finesse,
With each gentle, soul's caress.

Cascading Emotions

In winds that whisper secrets untold,
Hearts find solace in stories old,
Beneath the moon's soft and gentle light,
Dreams take flight in silent night.

Waves of laughter and tears collide,
In the ebb and flow of life's grand tide,
Moments of joy, moments of pain,
Emotions cascading like summer rain.

The stars bear witness to a lonesome sigh,
As fleeting memories drift and fly,
Through the corridors of time they sweep,
In the sacred spaces of the heart, they keep.

The sun rises, a new day to start,
Binding fragments of a fractured heart,
With every dawn, hope ignites and blooms,
Chasing away the night's gloomy rooms.

Emotions as deep as oceans wide,
In their depths, no truth can hide,
Through the highs and lows, the bitter and sweet,
Make us human, whole, complete.

Journey of the Heart

A path unfolds beneath our feet,
In the rhythm of life's pulsating beat,
Through valleys low and mountains high,
The heart embarks, learning to fly.

Whispers of love like gentle streams,
Carry us through the land of dreams,
Woven threads of fate and chance,
In the dance of life, a timeless trance.

Crimson sunsets warm the soul,
As the tides of time unyieldingly roll,
Echoes of laughter, whispers of sorrow,
Shape our past, present, and tomorrow.

Each step taken, a story unfurls,
In the endless journey of our worlds,
Where love's embrace dispels the night,
Guiding us towards eternal light.

In moments still, we find our way,
Through trials faced, come what may,
The heart's journey is a sacred art,
A timeless, ever-unfolding chart.

Flickers of Tenderness

In the quiet moments of the night,
Where the stars lend their gentle light,
Soft whispers of tender care,
Fill the air, sweet and rare.

A touch, a glance, a heartfelt sigh,
In these gestures, love does lie,
Flickers of tenderness, so bright,
Guide us through the darkest night.

Amidst the chaos, a calming breath,
In gentle kindness, we find our strength,
Through every storm, through every tear,
Tender love remains ever near.

In the cradle of compassionate grace,
We find our refuge, our sacred place,
Where hearts beat with a golden hue,
In every tender moment, love renews.

The simplest acts, in whispers shared,
Reveal the depths of how we care,
Flickers of tenderness, like stars above,
Illuminate the path of boundless love.

Nurturing Shadows

In the embrace of twilight's shade,
Where day fades and dreams are made,
Shadows dance with a tender grace,
In their folds, we find a quiet place.

The nurturing shadows gently fall,
Casting peace on hearts that call,
In their refuge, fears subside,
In their darkened arms, we safely hide.

Through the mysteries of night they weave,
Whispering secrets, tales they leave,
Guiding souls through fields unknown,
In nurturing shadows, we're never alone.

Under the canopy of the night's embrace,
We find a solace, a tranquil space,
A world where shadows softly kiss,
A sanctuary of silent bliss.

As dawn approaches, shadows fade,
But their nurturing gifts are humbly laid,
In every twilight, their presence stays,
A gentle reminder of love's serene ways.

Milton Keynes UK
Ingram Content Group UK Ltd.
UKHW050131130724
445613UK00003B/46

9 789916 861264